Houghton Mifflin
Reading

Reading Adventures

HOUGHTON MIFFLIN HARCOURT
School Publishers

"A Mr. Rubbish Mood" from *Judy Moody Saves the World* by Megan McDonald, illustrated by Peter Reynolds. Text copyright © 2002 by Megan McDonald. Illustrations copyright © 2002 by Peter Reynolds. Reprinted by permission of Candlewick Press Inc. and Megan McDonald.

"My Favorite Pet" and "My Smelly Pet" from *Judy Moody* by Megan McDonald, illustrated by Peter Reynolds. Text copyright © 2000 by Megan McDonald. Illustrations copyright © 2000 by Peter Reynolds. Reprinted by permission of Candlewick Press Inc. and Megan McDonald.

Copyright © 2012 by Houghton Mifflin Harcourt Publishing Company

All rights reserved. No part of this work may be reproduced or transmitted in any form or by any means, electronic or mechanical, including photocopying or recording, or by any information storage and retrieval system, without the prior written permission of the copyright owner unless such copying is expressly permitted by federal copyright law. Requests for permission to make copies of any part of the work should be addressed to Houghton Mifflin Harcourt Publishing Company, Attn: Contracts, Copyrights, and Licensing, 9400 South Park Center Loop, Orlando, Florida 32819.

Printed in the U.S.A.

ISBN: 978-0-547-68604-2

2 3 4 5 6 7 8 9 10 0914 20 19 18 17 16 15 14 13 12 11

4500329760   A B C D E F G

> If you have received these materials as examination copies free of charge, Houghton Mifflin Harcourt Publishing Company retains title to the materials and they may not be resold. Resale of examination copies is strictly prohibited.

> Possession of this publication in print format does not entitle users to convert this publication, or any portion of it, into electronic format.

READING Adventures

Theme 1

The Robodogs of Greenville 4
by Thomas S. Park

Activity Central
Tell Me When, Tell Me Where 12

Activity Central
You've Got Something to Say! 13

Your Turn
First, Next, Last 14

Theme 2

The Young Man, the Hawk, and the Raven 16
retold by Laura Layton Strom

Ram's Angry Horns 20
retold by Myka-Lynne Sokoloff

Activity Central
Read It! Record It! 30

Your Turn
Make a Connection 32

Theme 3

Lights, Camera, Action! The History of Movies 34
by Chris Bennett

Activity Central
Media Maze 42

Your Turn
What Happens in the End? 44

Theme 4

Forests 46
by Mark Goldberg

What Is a Rain Forest? 52

Activity Central
Pleased, Happy, or Thrilled? 58

Your Turn
Let's Make Something Very Clear 60

Theme 5

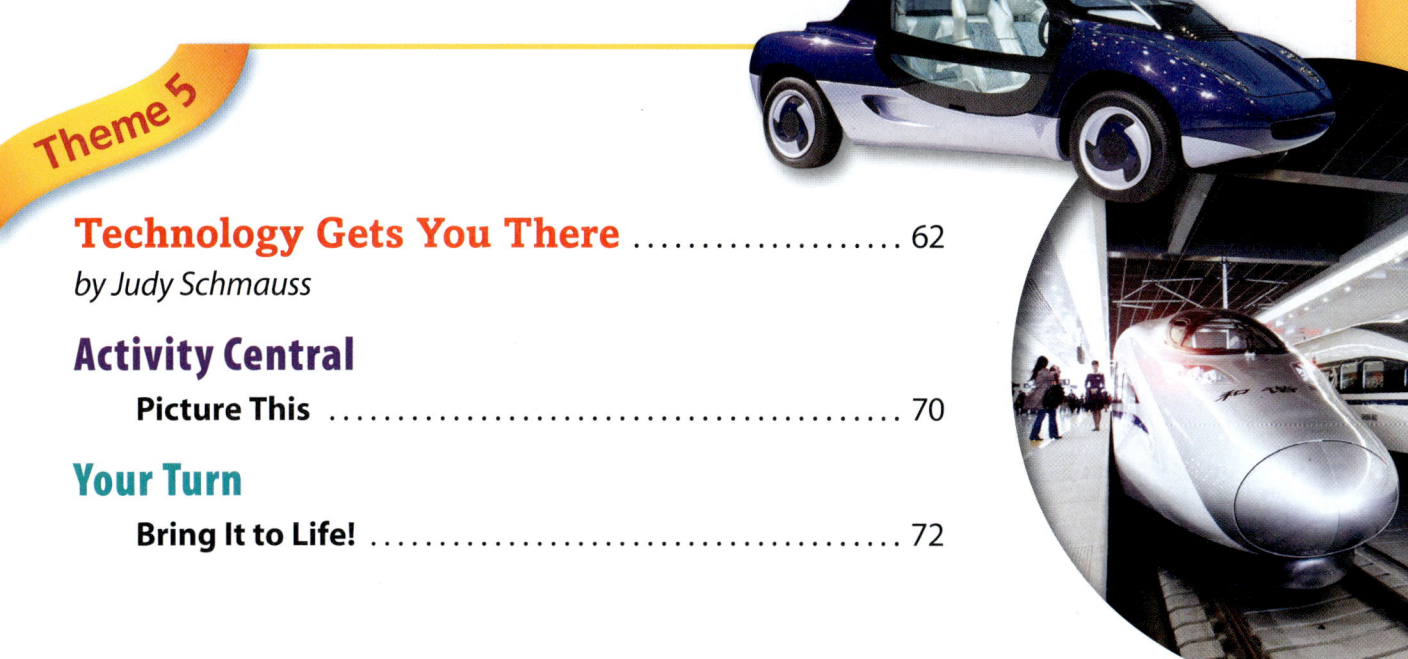

Technology Gets You There 62
by Judy Schmauss

Activity Central
    Picture This 70

Your Turn
    Bring It to Life! 72

Theme 6

"A Mr. Rubbish Mood"
from Judy Moody Saves the World! 74
by Megan McDonald

"My Favorite Pet" and "My Smelly Pet"
from Judy Moody 88
by Megan McDonald

Activity Central
    Defined Online 104

Your Turn
    Linked Together 106

The ROBODOGS of Greenville

by Thomas S. Park   illustrated by John Hovell

Characters

| Narrator | Cosmo | Professor |
| Diz | Robodog | Captain Spacely |

SCENE 1
Setting: Diz's house

Narrator: This story takes place in the year 2222 in a small town called Greenville. Greenville is a friendly little community, just like many other towns. Everyone gets along there.

Diz: Hi, Cosmo! Thanks for coming over.

Cosmo: Anytime, Diz! How are things over at your dad's hydro car store?

Diz: Really busy, Cosmo.

Cosmo: I hear they're selling those hydro cars faster than the factory on planet Mars can make them!

Narrator: Diz and Cosmo live with their families in Greenville. Their parents fly the children to school in the family hydro cars. The children chat with their friends each evening on the family televideocomputers. They also play with their family dogs.

Diz: Here, Robodog! Catch the flying disk!

Robodog: I am coming, Owner Diz. I will catch the disk.

Narrator: There is one unusual thing about the dogs in Greenville. All the dogs are robots.

Diz: Good catch, Robodog.

Robodog: Thank you, Owner Diz. What can I do for you now?

Narrator: The robodog is the only kind of dog in Greenville. Scientists have built robodogs to be better than real dogs. They can speak. They can take care of chores such as cleaning and cooking. They can even beam movies from their eyes onto a wall.

Cosmo: Last night, our robodog showed us an old movie.
Diz: What was it about?
Cosmo: It was about a real dog. She was beautiful!
Diz: A real dog? What was she like?
Cosmo: A lot like our robodogs. She could do tricks and help her owners.
Diz: Could she speak?
Cosmo: She could only make a sound called barking. She didn't know any human words.
Diz: Really? That's strange.
Robodog: Yes. That is very strange, Owner Diz.
Cosmo: Robodog, I'm hungry. Would you go to the kitchen and make sandwiches for Diz and me, please?
Robodog: I will be right back, Owner Diz and Friend Cosmo.

Cosmo: The dog in the movie seemed to love her owner. She was sweet and cuddly. She didn't just work around the house.

Diz: The dog loved her owner? I wish my robodog were like that.

Narrator: You see, robodogs are helpful and can do tricks, but they are not sweet or cuddly.

Cosmo: Maybe we should talk to the professor about this.

SCENE 2
Setting: The professor's house

Narrator: The professor is an expert on animals. So Diz and Cosmo go to talk to the professor about the differences between real dogs and robodogs.

Professor: Yes, Diz and Cosmo. It's true that real dogs could be happy or sad. They could even show love.

Diz: Why don't our robodogs show emotion?

Professor: Scientists don't know how to make dogs that act like friends. They can make them useful, but not loving.

Cosmo: My robodog cleans my room, makes my meals, and helps me with my homework.

Diz: Robodogs aren't very cuddly!

Cosmo: I know. After Robodog has done its chores or tricks, it just switches off.

Professor: That's right. It dozes. The scientists made robodogs that way to save energy.

Diz: I wish I had a real dog.

Cosmo: There aren't any more real dogs. They disappeared permanently from Earth a hundred years ago.

Professor: It's funny that you should say that. I just got off my Intergalactic Computer Phone with the famous explorer Captain Spacely. He told me about an astonishing discovery. Maybe he can tell you about it, too. Computer Phone, call Captain Spacely.

Spacely: Captain Spacely here. Professor, do you want to hear more about my discovery?

Professor: Yes, indeed I do, Captain. Tell my friends Diz and Cosmo what you have found.

Spacely: I can do better than that. I'll show them what I've found!

Narrator: Captain Spacely steps away from the computer phone. Diz and Cosmo hear a whining sound. Then they hear barking.

Diz: What is that strange sound?

Cosmo: I heard that sound in the movie. It's the barking sound a real dog makes!

Narrator: Captain Spacely is visible on the screen again. He beckons to a furry thing that leaps into his arms. Cosmo and Diz see that it looks something like a robodog, but it acts differently.

Spacely: I've found real dogs! There is a small planet that has many of the same animals that were once on Earth. In fact, it has so many kinds of animals that food and space are becoming hard to find.

Narrator: The dog in Captain Spacely's arms wags its tail and licks his face. Diz and Cosmo look at the dog with amazement.

Diz: I wish I could have one of those dogs!

Cosmo: Me, too!

Professor: I think that can be arranged. Tell them your plan, Captain Spacely!

Spacely: To help the animals, I am bringing a spaceship full of dogs back to Earth! There is lots of room on Earth for dogs. Cosmo and Diz, if you promise to care for them, you can have the first two!

Diz and Cosmo: Thanks, Captain Spacely!

> **SCENE 3**
> **Setting:** Diz's house

Narrator: Sure enough, Captain Spacely brings real dogs back to Earth. Cosmo and Diz get the first two dogs.

Diz: Give me a hug, Scooter!

Cosmo: Here, Rascal! Come and play with me!

Narrator: As for the robodogs, Cosmo and Diz decide to keep them. They come in handy when it is time to give Scooter and Rascal a bath.

Robodog: Owner Cosmo, should I get Rascal's bath ready?

Cosmo: Yes, Robodog. After that, would you take Rascal out for a walk?

Activity Central
Tell Me When Tell Me Where

When you tell about something that happened, it is important to use words that tell **when** events happened. Time-order words such as *before*, *after,* and *then* help your listener understand the order of events.

After Robodog has done its chores or tricks, it just switches off.

What word in the sentence above helps you understand when Robodog switches off?

To give your listeners a clear picture, you also need to include words that tell **where** things are or where they happened.

Would you go to the kitchen and make sandwiches for Diz and me, please?

What words in the sentence above tell you where Robodog goes?

With a partner, take turns telling about an event in *The Robodogs of Greenville*, using words that tell when and where.

You've Got Something to Say!

When you have discussions with your classmates about stories you have read, do you know what to say? Here are some ways to make discussions fun and helpful.

Before the Discussion
- Reread the story. Then think about these questions.

Fiction	Nonfiction
Who is your favorite character? Why? How is the problem solved?	What are the important ideas? What information interested you the most?

During the Discussion
- Add your ideas to what someone else is saying.
- Stick to the main topic.

Read what these students are saying about *The Robodogs of Greenville*. Then have your own discussion about the play.

I liked the inventions in the future, like flying cars.

My favorite invention was the robodog, because it shows movies.

Yes. I would like a dog that shows movies!

Your Turn: First, Next, Last

Good writers use time-order words and phrases, such as *before, after, then,* and *last week,* to help their readers understand the order of events in their writing.

In *The Robodogs of Greenville,* Cosmo and Diz are surprised that Captain Spacely discovered real dogs on another planet. Later, they are even more surprised when they receive the first two real dogs. The letter below is about another surprise. How do the time-order words and phrases in the letter help you understand the order of events?

Dear Justin,

You won't believe what happened to me last week! My mom left me clues for a treasure hunt. First, I had to go to the living room. Next, I had to go to the kitchen. Finally, I had to go to the basement. After a few seconds, I heard a funny sound. I walked toward the sound, where I found a new kitten waiting for me. I named the kitten Mia. I hope you will be able to meet her soon.

Sincerely,
Kayla

Reflect on Your Writing

Look back at the personal narrative you have written in this theme. As you look over your writing, ask yourself these questions.

✓ Is it easy to understand the order of events in my writing?

✓ Where should I add words that tell about time order, such as *before*, *after*, *then*, or *last week*?

✓ Can I add any of the new words I learned from stories I have read?

Answer the questions and then edit your writing.

Theme 2

The Young Man, the Hawk, and the Raven

A Bidpai Fable from India

retold by Laura Layton Strom
illustrated by Micha Archer

A young man named Nandin was wandering in the forest one morning. As Nandin rounded some tall bamboo plants, he saw a beautiful Hawk circling above a tall tree. He heard a baby bird chirp not far away. He looked toward the noise and saw a hungry baby raven, alone in Hawk's nest.

Hawk swooped down and landed next to Raven. Hawk had a piece of meat in her bill. She tore the meat into pieces and began feeding Raven. Nandin shouted out, "Hawk, what are you doing?"

"I'm feeding Raven, who has lost his mother," replied Hawk.

"Why are you feeding baby Raven?" asked Nandin.

"He is hungry," Hawk said. With that, Hawk flew away to get more food.

Nandin thought for some time about this. "So this young bird must only chirp and food arrives? This lazy creature is quite clever not to work," Nandin said to himself. "I will be clever, too."

"From now on, instead of working hard, I will stay quietly at home. Surely someone will take care of me, just as Hawk takes care of Raven. A man is much more important than a raven!"

Nandin went home and sat in his favorite chair. He waited hopefully for someone to come to his house and bring him food. By afternoon his stomach was rumbling because he was hungry. No one came near his home all day long. Nandin was very hungry by the end of the day. As soon as night fell, Nandin fell fast asleep.

Nandin awoke the second morning with an empty stomach, but he was still determined to wait for someone to take care of him. "Maybe if I sit near the window and make noise like Raven someone will come," he thought.

From time to time, Nandin yelled out the window, "Feed me!" Still no one came near his house. By the end of the day, he was very hungry indeed.

Nandin awoke on the third day feeling achy and angry. He was very hungry, thin, and feeling weak. He sat by his window all day long, calling out, "Feed me! Feed me!" Still no one came to him.

"Why does no one see that I am weak and hungry? I am calling out to be fed just like Raven. Why does no one help me?" he wondered.

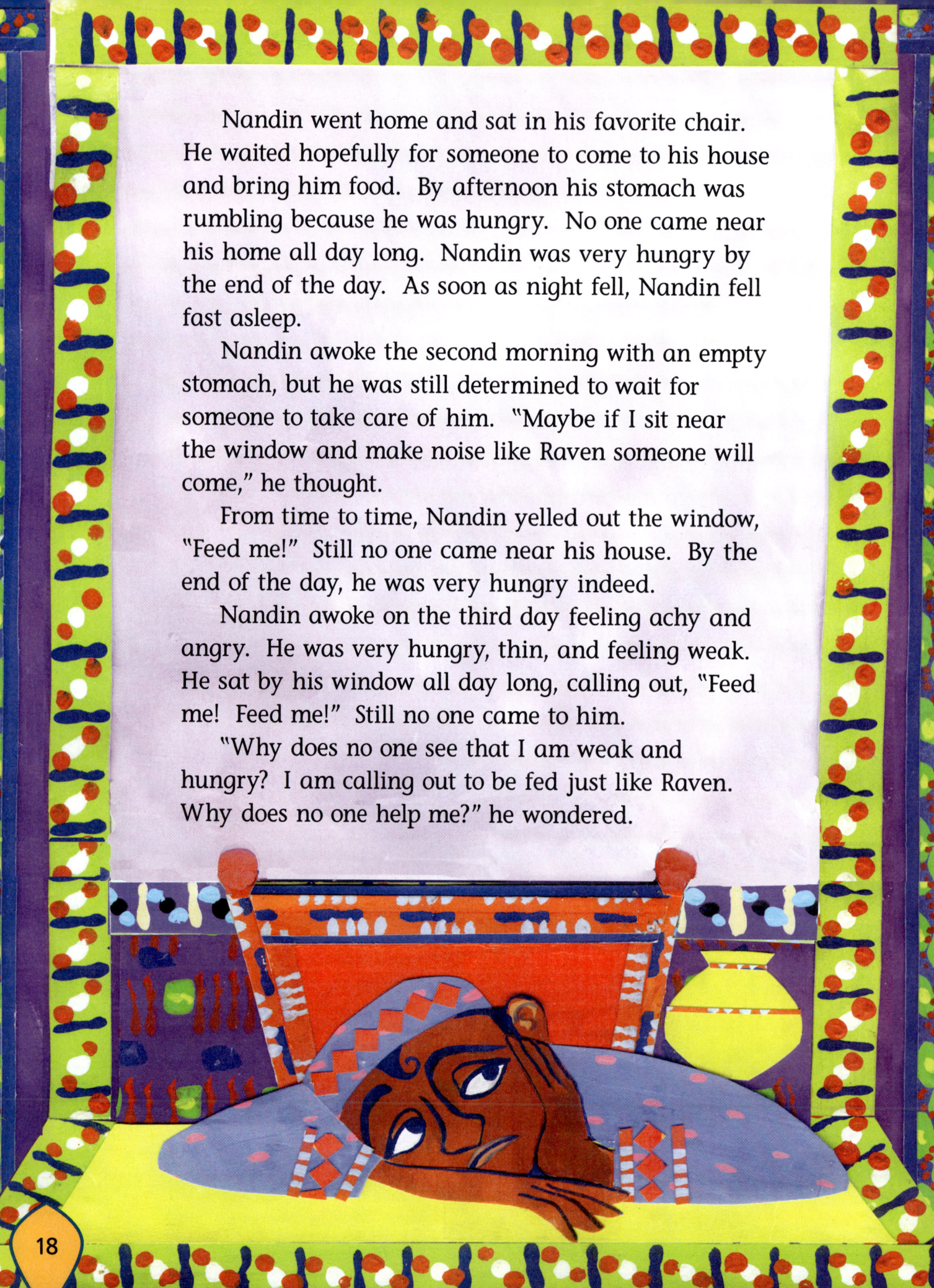

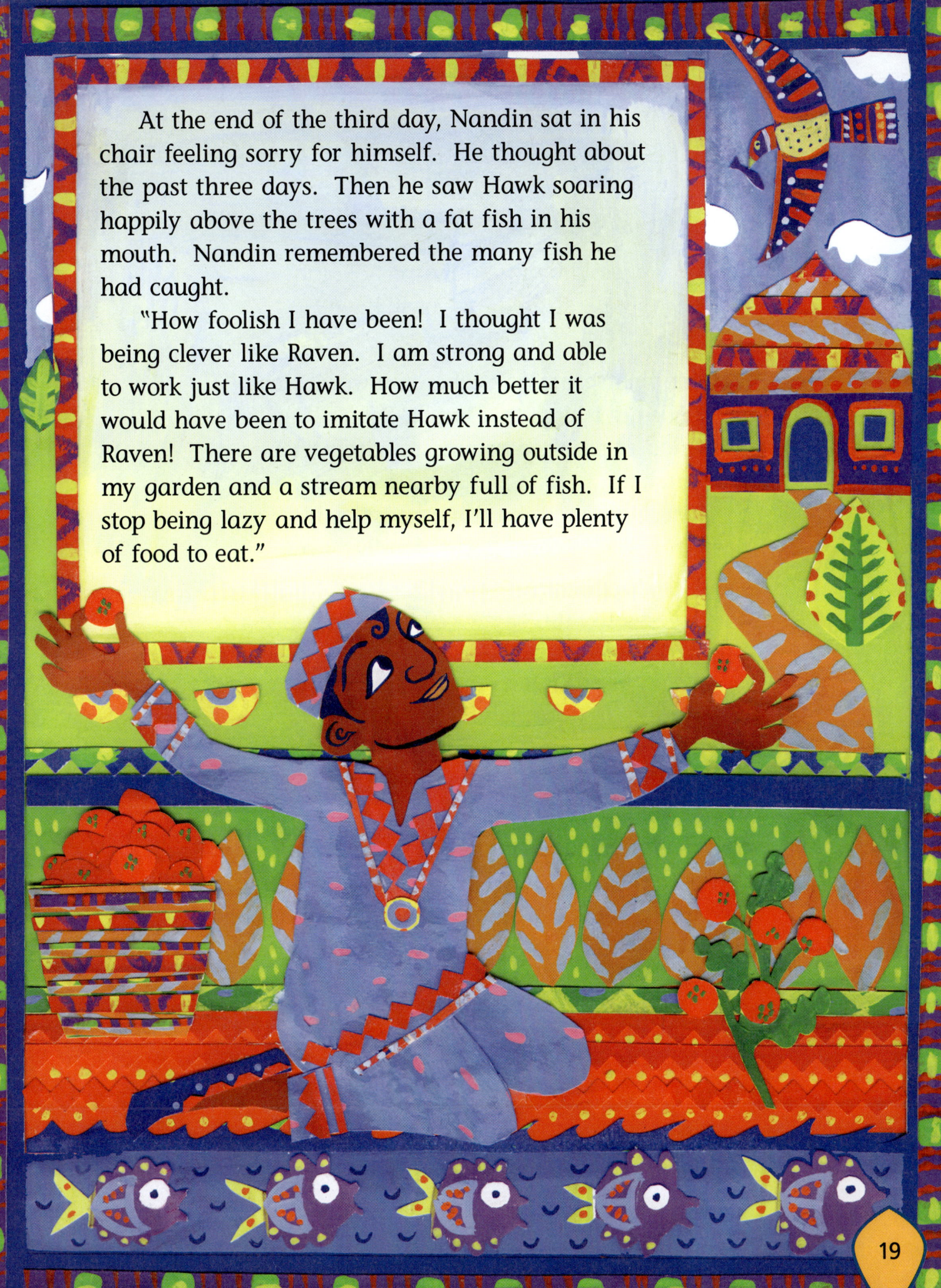

At the end of the third day, Nandin sat in his chair feeling sorry for himself. He thought about the past three days. Then he saw Hawk soaring happily above the trees with a fat fish in his mouth. Nandin remembered the many fish he had caught.

"How foolish I have been! I thought I was being clever like Raven. I am strong and able to work just like Hawk. How much better it would have been to imitate Hawk instead of Raven! There are vegetables growing outside in my garden and a stream nearby full of fish. If I stop being lazy and help myself, I'll have plenty of food to eat."

Ram's Angry Horns
A Myth from Nigeria

retold by Myka-Lynne Sokoloff
illustrated by Cindy Revell

◆◆◆◆◆◆◆◆◆◆◆◆◆◆◆◆◆◆◆◆◆◆◆◆◆

One fine spring day, when the world was new, Ewe gave birth to a lamb. Soon all of the villagers crowded around to admire her new lamb.

"What a handsome thing he is!" said Leopard. Gazelle also looked fondly at the young lamb.

"It's good to have new life in the village," said Elephant.

Hyena joked, "One day soon lamb will be running around the village, butting into everyone's business." The villagers all chuckled at the remark. No one knew how true Hyena's words would turn out to be.

Finally, the villagers left the new mother to rest with her lamb. "You will be called Ram," Ewe baaed softly. "You are the handsomest baby in all of Africa!"

Indeed, the lamb became more and more handsome as he grew. In fact, he was so handsome that he seemed to get his way with everyone, especially his mother. Ram thought only about himself. He never stopped to think about others.

In time, the other young animals in the village became very put out with Ram. They no longer wanted to play with him. When they saw Ram, the other animal children ran and hid.

Each day, from morning till night, Ram raced around the village causing trouble. Ram splashed in the water. He sprayed drops of water on Hyena, who lounged in the sun on the shore. Ram hopped across the river stones. Then he ran boldly up and down Crocodile's back, from the tip of Crocodile's tail to the very end of his nose! He ran through the fields where others had just planted seeds. He rubbed his muddy coat against the clean laundry that hung on the line. He tracked mud through the hut where his mother had just swept the floor.

Ewe looked up from her chores. She saw all the mischief Ram was making. She baaed gently to make her son stop. He just pretended not to hear her. Ewe bleated and cried more strongly. Soon she was bellowing deeply and loudly. Ram continued to ignore his mother.

Ram had no friends. His mother didn't know what to do with her selfish child. She wished he would learn some manners, but she had spoiled him beyond repair. Each time Ram misbehaved, the villagers shivered. They waited nervously for Ewe's loud bellows to begin.

Zebra covered her ears. Elephant winced in pain. Crocodile swam away. Flamingo flapped her wings wildly. Hyena would have laughed, but he didn't find Ram's tricks funny.

As Ram grew, so did the disasters he created. When a villager scolded him for his actions, Ram lowered his horns and stamped his feet. Then he found new ways to annoy his neighbors.

Finally, the villagers had had enough. They could stand Ram's actions and his mother's loud scolding no longer. One night they met under a full moon at the watering hole.

"Ram thinks of no one but himself," complained Zebra. "We must teach him a lesson!"

Flamingo fluttered her feathers. "My ears ache from the noise. Ram's mother should learn a lesson as well!"

Elephant nodded wisely. "It's his mother's fault. She has spoiled Ram since the day he was born! Now not even she can control her son, no matter how loudly she bellows."

"We have no choice," Baboon said. "We must send Ram and his mother away from the village. Otherwise, our homes and our children will constantly be in harm's way."

Soon the villagers agreed on a solution. They packed up Ram, his mother, and their belongings. They all formed a parade to escort Ram and Ewe to the edge of town. Ewe and Ram were to speak to no one in the village again.

"Ah, quiet," sighed Leopard as he lay down to doze in the soft, flat grass.

"Now we can get some rest," thought Elephant. It had been so long, she had nearly forgotten what a nice nap felt like.

"Peace at last," said Crocodile, grinning widely in the river.

The peace did not last long. Ram felt lonely. He was bored, too. Ewe could control her son no better than she could in the village.

One day Ram pawed at the dirt. He kicked the grass. Ram got angrier and angrier, feeling sorry for himself.

As Ram stared at the ground, he noticed something shiny. It was a piece of glass. An idea popped into his head. He knew how he would get even with the animals in the village!

Ram held the glass so that it caught the sun's rays. It shone brightly on a clump of dried grass. Very quickly, the grass grew warm. Finally, it began to burn. Ram blew on the little flame with all his might.

Next, Ram shook his horned head as fast as he could to make the flames grow higher. He stood back and rubbed his hooves together with glee.

The flames raced toward the village. The fire burned up the grass where Leopard napped in the warm sun. Leopard escaped just in time! The flames licked the leafy trees where Cheetah liked to climb. Fortunately, Cheetah was off doing laundry at the river, so he wasn't hurt. Soon the fire dashed toward the huts in the heart of the village.

"I smell smoke," Hyena giggled nervously.

Flamingo pointed one wing at the ball of fire that headed straight in their direction.

"Quick, everyone! We must do something!" screamed Baboon.

Elephant trumpeted to call the villagers together. Then she raced to the watering hole. She filled her trunk to spray the flames. The other villagers carried baskets and gourds of water to put out the fire. By the time they finished, the watering hole was nearly dry. When night fell, the flames were out. Little remained of the village. Once again, the villagers met under the full moon.

"We put up with Ram's tricks when he was young," Leopard complained. "His mother just got noisier and noisier. We covered our ears to block the sound."

Baboon nodded. "Now Ram has ruined our food and burned our homes."

"We must send Ram and his mother even farther away," Elephant said. The villagers agreed, sadly. They did not want to harm their neighbors.

The villagers put their heads together and came up with a plan. They used a fallen tree trunk to build a giant seesaw. Ram and Ewe stood on one end. Elephant and Cheetah jumped on the other end. Ram and his mother flew high up into the clouds.

Now you may be wondering what happened to Ram and his mother. If you look and listen carefully next time a thunderstorm comes, you will find the answer in the sky.

Those lightning bolts? That's Ram tossing balls of fire around the sky with his angry horns. That noise you call thunder? That's his mother, bellowing at her naughty son.

The sky will be their home forever. For that is where they belong, far away from the village, where they would surely make more trouble!

Activity Central
Read It! Record It!

Stories, such as *Ram's Angry Horns* and *The Young Man, the Hawk, and the Raven*, were first told by parents to their children or by storytellers a very long time ago.

Did you ever listen to a storyteller or to a story read aloud on a CD or podcast? These stories are told or read by someone who has practiced to make the story fun to listen to.

Choose a story or poem to read aloud.

1. Read the story or poem aloud a few times. Try out some different voices to make your characters come alive. Don't read too fast or too slowly.

2. Once you have practiced reading the story or poem, make a recording.

3. Listen to the recording, and make sure you like the way it sounds. If it's not as good as you would like, record it again.

4. Draw some pictures to make the details of the story or poem clear to your listeners.

Then play your recording for your class and display your pictures. If your teacher has a class website, you may be able to post your recording and pictures for your friends and family to enjoy. Get ready to take a bow!

Be sure you
- speak clearly.
- vary your speed.
- use lots of expression.

Your Turn: Make a Connection

When you write compare and contrast paragraphs, you organize your ideas to make them clear for your readers. In one paragraph, tell how two people, places, or things are alike. In the second paragraph, tell how they are different.

Make your ideas clear by showing your readers how your ideas are connected. How might you use the linking words below to connect ideas?

- also
- another
- and
- more
- but

How does this writer use linking words?

How Are Elephants Like Zebras?

Elephants and zebras are similar in many ways. Both animals live on the grasslands of Africa. Zebras live in large herds. Elephants live in groups, too. Both zebras and elephants are also part of small family groups. They look out for one another. Another way they are similar is their diet. Elephants eat grass, plants, seeds, twigs, bark, and fruit. Zebras also eat grass.

Reflect on Your Writing

Look back at the compare and contrast paragraphs you wrote in Theme 2. Ask yourself these questions:

- Did I begin each paragraph with a topic sentence?
- Did I group the ways my subjects are alike in the paragraph that compares?
- Did I group the ways the subjects are different in the paragraph that contrasts?
- Where can I add linking words so that my ideas are connected and clear to the reader?

Find ways to revise your paragraphs so your readers can see how your ideas are linked.

Theme 3

LIGHTS, CAMERA, ACTION!
The History of Movies
by Chris Bennett

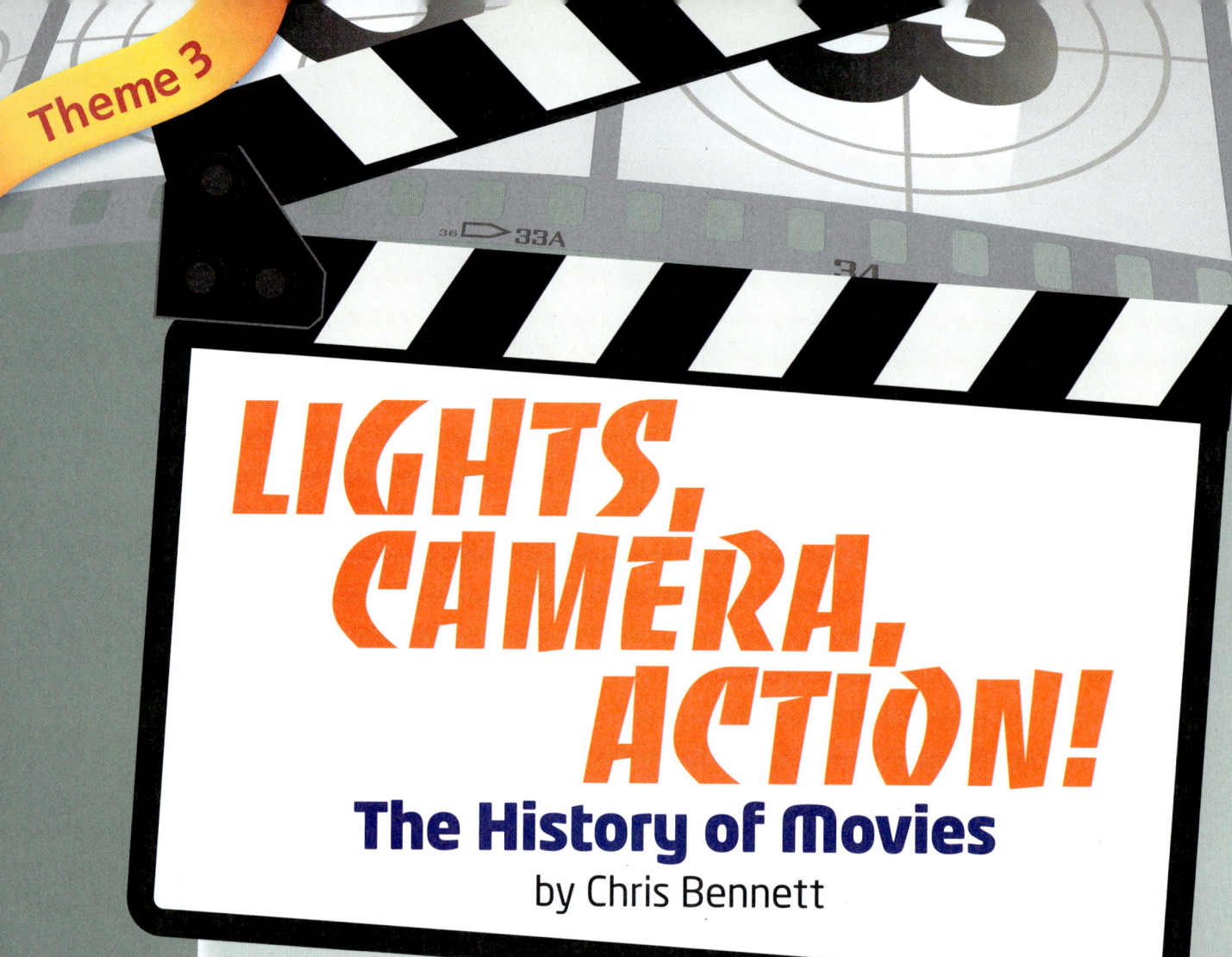

Lights, camera, action! When you hear those words you think of movies. Just over one hundred years ago, movies were very different than they are today.

The first motion pictures in the late 1800s were black-and-white moving pictures with no sound. They were only about a minute long. The early inventors worked hard to make moving pictures better. They designed new cameras to take pictures and record them on film. They designed projectors to show the pictures. Their designs and ideas led to today's movies. Today's movies are the most exciting and amazing movies ever!

Edison's Kinetoscope

The very first step toward making movies was the invention of photography in the 1820s. Photography is the process of making pictures with a camera. After the invention of photography, inventors wanted a way to show movement. The race was on!

One of the first people to succeed was an American, Thomas Edison. In 1889, he and his assistant, William Dickson, invented the kinetoscope. The kinetoscope used a camera, film, and an electric lamp.

Inside a four-foot high wooden box, a loop of film ran through a special camera. An electric lamp under the film lit images on the film as it passed through the camera. Our eyes see the quick movement of the images as motion. A peephole at the top of the box allowed a single person to view the moving pictures. Later, in the 1890s, the public watched motion pictures for the very first time in kinetoscope parlors.

Thomas Edison

In the 1890s, kinetoscope parlors opened all across the United States. At a parlor, a customer could view a different film in five different kinetoscopes for five cents each.

The Lumières' Motion-Picture Projector

Auguste and Louis Lumière

In Paris, Charles Antoine Lumière saw a movie through Edison's kinetoscope. He was impressed, but he believed his sons could design a better way to watch movies. His sons, Auguste and Louis, were two of the smartest scientists in Paris. They noticed one big problem with Edison's kinetoscope. Only one person could view the film at a time.

The Lumière brothers invented a camera and a projector that was one machine. They called their invention a *cinematographe*. The *cinematographe* recorded images on film. These images could be projected onto a screen. Now many people could sit together and watch larger moving images. The Lumières showed their movies to the public much like movie theaters do today.

This new entertainment was different and exciting. Nothing like it had ever been seen before!

The Lumière brothers presented their first motion-picture show in December 1895. Soon, they were showing their motion pictures in cities all over the world.

Nickelodeon storefront theater from the early 1900s

Early Movies and Movie Theaters

Soon, smaller, lighter movie projectors were being made in the United States. Movies became part of fairgrounds and "traveling tent" shows all over the country. The moving pictures had no sound. Narrators and musicians often traveled with the shows. They told the story and added music and sound effects to the moving pictures.

The first movie theaters in the United States were called *nickelodeons*. These small theaters charged a nickel to watch a movie. Movies, called *shorts*, were only about fifteen minutes long. In a nickelodeon, a piano player often played along to the film as the audience watched.

In 1902, *A Trip to the Moon* was one of the first movies that told a story.

What Next? Sound!

Even though there was no sound, movies became more and more popular. In silent films, an actor's words were printed on the film and projected onto the screen. They were like words on a page.

The next challenge was to have sound. People wanted to hear movies as well as see them. Moviemakers had always been interested in sound. In 1919, a new kind of film made sound on film possible. A camera recorded images and sound on film at the same time. At first, the quality of the sound was poor. After many experiments, the quality improved. Then big movie theaters started buying expensive sound systems. The public was very excited to hear what the actors were saying.

The new movies with sound were called *talkies*. The first full-length talkie was *The Jazz Singer* in 1927. The movie had both music and speaking. It was a smash success! Movies would never be silent again.

The Jazz Singer was the first feature film with dialogue and music.

The Wizard of Oz had lots of color!

Color Films

Another big step in the history of movies was adding color to film. Just as with sound, making movies with a lot of color took some time to get right. At first, in some early movies, color was painted onto film, frame by frame. Imagine a hand-painted film! Or film was tinted by dipping it into dye.

By the 1930s, a better process had been invented. It used three layers of special color film. Each layer of film was a separate color. Together, they made all the colors.

One of the first color movies using the new process was *The Wizard of Oz* in 1939. This movie still looks great! Later, less expensive color film and cameras were designed.

Special Effects

For most of their history, movies have had special effects. These are tricks that make things seem different than they really are. Moviemakers can do amazing things with special effects.

Blue screen photography is a common special effect. Using blue screens, an actor can seem to be at the top of the Empire State Building or flying over the Grand Canyon. The trick is that the actor never leaves the movie studio!

How does it happen? First, the actor is filmed in front of a blue screen. Next, a film of a background, such as the Grand Canyon, is made. Then the two pieces of film are put together to look like one very real scene.

Another special effect is called *slow motion*. A slow-motion camera films action at a faster speed than normal. When a projector plays the film at normal speed, the action appears to slow down.

This actor is posing in front of a blue screen.

Today, most movie special effects are done using high-tech video cameras and computers. In 1993, *Jurassic Park* brought dinosaurs to life in a way that wowed audiences. In 1995, the film *Jumanji* made the jungle animals in Chris Van Allsburg's book seem very real. Later, *Avatar* showed life on an imaginary planet in new ways. These movies could never have been made at an earlier time. In fact, the whole movie experience has changed so much in just the last twenty years.

Now in some theaters, you can watch a 3-D movie with surround sound. Your seat moves back to view the action on a dome screen seventy-two feet high!

Movies have come a long way since the silent movie shorts of the nickelodeon. Today's movies are much more thrilling than the first silent movies.

The movie *Godzilla* was made in 1954. It had great special effects for a movie of its time, and it was a big hit with adult audiences. Forty years later, *Jurassic Park* thrilled moviegoers with lifelike dinosaurs.

Activity Central
Media Maze

When your parents went to school and wanted to find information on a topic, they may have read books, newspapers, and magazines. Today there are many other ways to find information.

Suppose you wanted to research movie special effects. You could still use books, magazines, or newspapers. You could also use many different kinds of media for your research. You could

- search the Internet for websites about special effects.
- watch a video clip of a makeup artist working with an actor.
- study charts and graphs that give information about numbers or dates related to special effects.
- watch a TV show about the history of special effects.

As you explore different types of media, look for the main ideas and details in the information you find. This will help you understand and organize the information.

Media Presentations

1. Work with a partner or a small group. Choose and research a topic related to movies, such as silent movies, special effects, or cartoons.

2. Choose a type of media mentioned on the previous page to find information on your topic.

3. Note the main ideas and details in the material you select.

4. Present your findings to the class. Be sure to explain clearly the main ideas and details in your presentation.

5. Include a picture, a chart, a graph, or a short video clip to help support your presentation.

What Happens in the End?

A good story makes it easy for the reader to get to know the characters and what happens to them. A good story has a problem and gets the reader interested in how the characters solve the problem. Good writers make sure to tell how the problem is solved.

Think about the stories you read in this theme. They were fun to read because they each had interesting characters that had to solve a problem. What was the problem in each story? What happened at the end? Did the ending of each story tell how the problem was solved?

Reflect on Your Writing

Look back at the story you wrote in this theme. Ask yourself these questions:

- What problem do the characters have?

- Did I organize the events in an order that makes sense?

- Is the problem solved in the end?

If you answer no to any of the questions, edit your story.

FORESTS

by Mark Goldberg

Types of Forests

You probably know that a forest is an area in which the main plants are trees. However, animals and many other kinds of plants also live in forests.

Forests grow in many parts of the world. Some forests are named for the types of trees that grow in them. Other forests are named for the area in which they grow.

Each type of forest needs a certain amount of rainfall and sunshine. Each forest also has certain temperatures that let it grow best. If any of these things change, the kinds of plants that grow in the forest may also change.

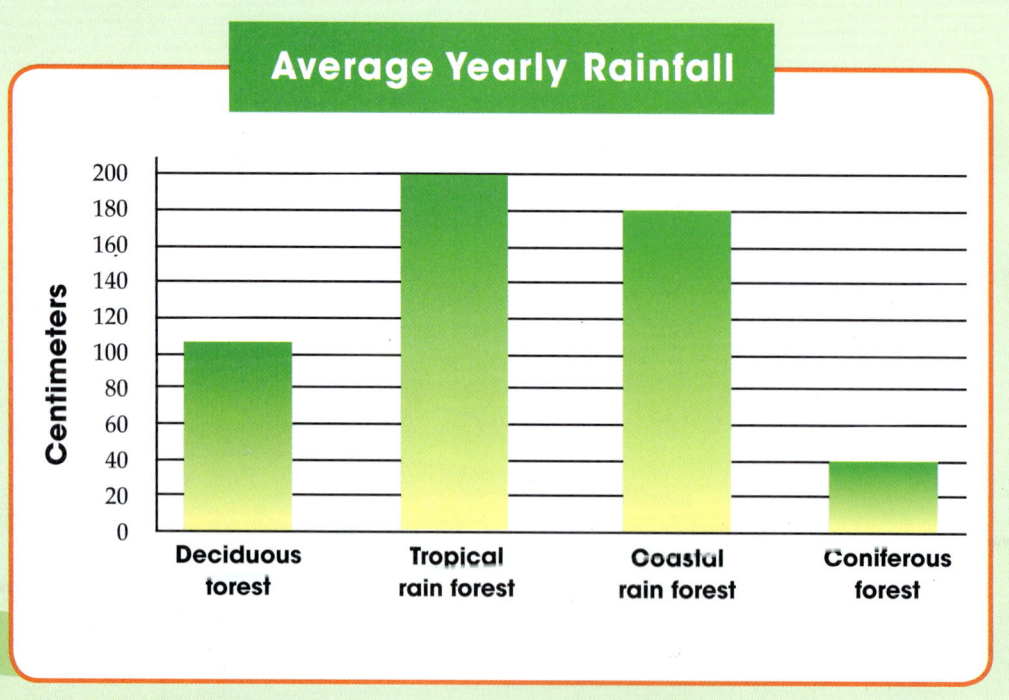

Deciduous Forests

Some trees, such as maples and oaks, have large, flat leaves that drop off each fall. New leaves grow back in the spring. Trees that lose and regrow their leaves each year are called deciduous (dee•SIH•joo•uhs) trees. Forests made up mostly of these trees are deciduous forests. They grow in places that have warm, wet summers and cold winters.

Deciduous leaves change color before they drop in the fall. When a deciduous tree drops its leaves, it needs less water. This helps the tree live through the winter, when water may be frozen.

The deciduous forest is a habitat for many kinds of living things, such as ferns, shrubs, and mosses. Animals such as insects, spiders, snakes, frogs, birds, rabbits, deer, and bears also live here.

spring   summer   fall   winter

Tropical Rain Forests

Tropical rain forests grow in places such as Hawaii and Costa Rica. These places are hot and wet all year. The trees grow very tall, and their leaves stay green all year.

More types of living things live in rain forests than anywhere else on Earth. Plants and animals make their homes in all the layers of the forest, from the tops of the trees to the ground.

Layers of the Rain Forest

A tropical rain forest has different layers. The top layer is the *canopy*. It is the tops of the tall trees. Below the canopy is the *understory*. It is smaller trees and plants. The lowest layer is the *forest floor*. Many kinds of plants and animals make their homes in each layer.

Coastal Rain Forests

Coastal rain forests grow where there is a lot of rain. Unlike a tropical rain forest, a coastal forest grows where it does not get too warm or too cold. Like tropical rain forests, coastal forests are thick with many kinds of tall trees. Coastal forests have the same kinds of layers as tropical rain forests.

1. The leaves of the canopy gets lots of water and sunlight. Many animals drink the water that collects on the leaves.

2. Understory plants get less sunlight and water than those in the canopy. Orchids, mosses, and ferns grow on the trunks of the tall trees.

3. Little sunlight reaches the forest floor. Plants that grow here do not need much light.

Coniferous Forests

What kind of trees would you find where there are very cold winters and cool summers? Mostly, you would find conifers (KAHN•uh•ferz)—trees that form seeds in cones. Conifers have needle-like leaves. Pines, spruces, and firs are common conifers. Conifers don't lose their needles in the fall. They stay green all year. This is why conifers are often called evergreens. Forests that contain mostly these kinds of trees are coniferous (koh•NIF•er•uhs) forests.

Conifers grow in areas that get less rain than other types of forests. The needle-shaped leaves of these trees help keep the trees from losing too much water.

Coniferous forests often have many lakes and streams. The trees, lakes, and streams provide habitats for many animals. Squirrels, moose, and wolves are common. Insects, such as mosquitoes and flies, also live in coniferous forests.

There are different types of forests. The main types of forests are deciduous forests, tropical rain forests, coastal rain forests, and coniferous forests. These forests provide habitats for many kinds of plants and animals.

Deciduous Forest

Tropical Rain Forest

Coastal Rain Forest

Coniferous Forest

What Is a Rain Forest?

A rain forest is a wet and warm place all year round. Most rain forests receive more than 100 inches of rain each year. The trees are evergreens. They grow very tall. Epiphyte (EP•uh•fyt) plants, or air plants, grow in rain forests. Epiphytes do not need soil to grow. They grow on other plants.

Canopy
A rain forest has different layers. The canopy is the top part of the rain forest. It is made up of the leaves and branches of the tallest trees.

Understory
The understory is the middle layer of the rain forest. Small trees and other plants are found here. They can live with little sunlight.

Forest Floor
The forest floor, or ground, is the bottom layer of the rain forest.

Types of Rain Forest

Tropical Rain Forest

A tropical rain forest is warm and humid most of the year. More rain falls here than in any other type of forest. The rain falls in heavy showers. In between the showers, lots of sunshine hits the top layer of the forest.

Coastal Rain Forest

Not all rain forests are tropical. Coastal, or temperate, rain forests are found near oceans. Temperatures in these forests are not too hot or too cold. The amount of rainfall in a coastal rain forest is similar to a tropical rain forest. There is less sunshine. Rain falls steadily most of the year. Sometimes fog, instead of rain, keeps the forest wet.

▲ Temperate rain forests are found near oceans.

The Giant Redwoods

One section of coastal rain forest in Northern California has giant redwood trees. These trees grow over 300 feet tall. They can live more than 1,000 years. The oldest redwood tree still standing is 2,200 years old!

Tropical Rain Forest Plants and Animals

Tropical rain forests are home to more types of plants and animals than any other places in the world. Birds, monkeys, bats, and butterflies live in the canopy at the tops of the tallest trees. Some of the birds that live here are eagles, macaws, and hummingbirds.

Macaw

Harpy Eagle

Hummingbird

The canopy layer is filled with amazing sights, sounds, and colors. Monkeys swing from thick vines. Colorful parrots and toucans perch and screech on long tree branches. Butterflies land on flowers. Snakes coil and sloths hang on branches.

Blue Morpho Butterfly

Howler Monkey

Sloth

Emerald Tree Boa

Toucan

| What Is a Rain Forest? | Types of Rain Forest | **Tropical Rain Forest Plants and Animals** |

Lots of different kinds of plants and animals live in the understory of a tropical rain forest. The understory is dark, wet, and hot. It is home to many kinds of insects. It is also home to frogs, snakes, and lizards. Large cats, such as jaguars, can be seen in the branches. They are looking for food.

Epiphytes, or air plants, such as orchids, mosses, and ferns, grow on the trees and other plants. Butterflies add color.

Many plants in the understory are used to make medicines. Scientists are still discovering new plants and animals in the rain forests.

Orchid

Stick Insect

Jaguar

Okapis

Pygmy Elephant

The largest animals live on the forest floor. In the rain forests of South America, jaguars, tapirs, and anteaters live. In the tropical rain forests of Africa, you will find leopards, okapis, and African forest elephants, or Pygmy elephants.

The Venus Flytrap

The floor of a tropical rain forest contains very few nutrients, or food, for plants. Plants that live there must find their own food. Venus flytrap plants have special leaves. A sweet-smelling material on the leaves attracts bugs. A bug lands on the leaf and the leaf closes over the bug. The plant then digests the bug. The plant uses the nutrients from the bug to grow!

Pleased, Happy, or Thrilled?

Some words, such as *pleased*, *happy*, and *thrilled*, have similar meanings. If you think about it, they are not exactly the same. When have you been pleased? happy? thrilled? Good writers and speakers choose words carefully so their audiences will understand exactly what they mean. Read the words under the line. Which word sounds the least certain? the most certain?

wonder — **think** — **believe** — **know**

Read the sentences below. What is the meaning of each underlined word?

- I <u>wonder</u> if we will see a red-headed woodpecker.
- I <u>believe</u> we will see one. Its red head is easy to spot.
- I <u>know</u> we are going to see lots of birds on this hike.

Copy the sentences below, filling in the blanks with words from the word bank. Then share your sentences with a partner. Ask your partner what word he or she chose for each sentence.

Word Bank

thrilled
happy
pleased
content
sorry
gloomy
sad
unhappy

I am __?__ that our hike is over.

Do you feel __?__ about the animals you saw?

I am __?__ because I saw some rabbits.

Your Turn

Let's Make Something Very Clear

Definitions

Good writers add definitions to explain the meaning of words that may not be familiar to their readers.

No Definition	Strong Definition
The soil of a tropical rain forest contains very few nutrients.	The soil of a tropical rain forest contains very few nutrients, or food, for plants.

Why is the strong definition better?

The word *nutrient* is explained within the sentence as food for plants.

Illustrations

Good writers also make their meaning clear by adding illustrations to their writing. Illustrations help explain and add new information to what they write.

What types of illustrations were included in the selections about the forests? How did the illustrations help you understand the information?

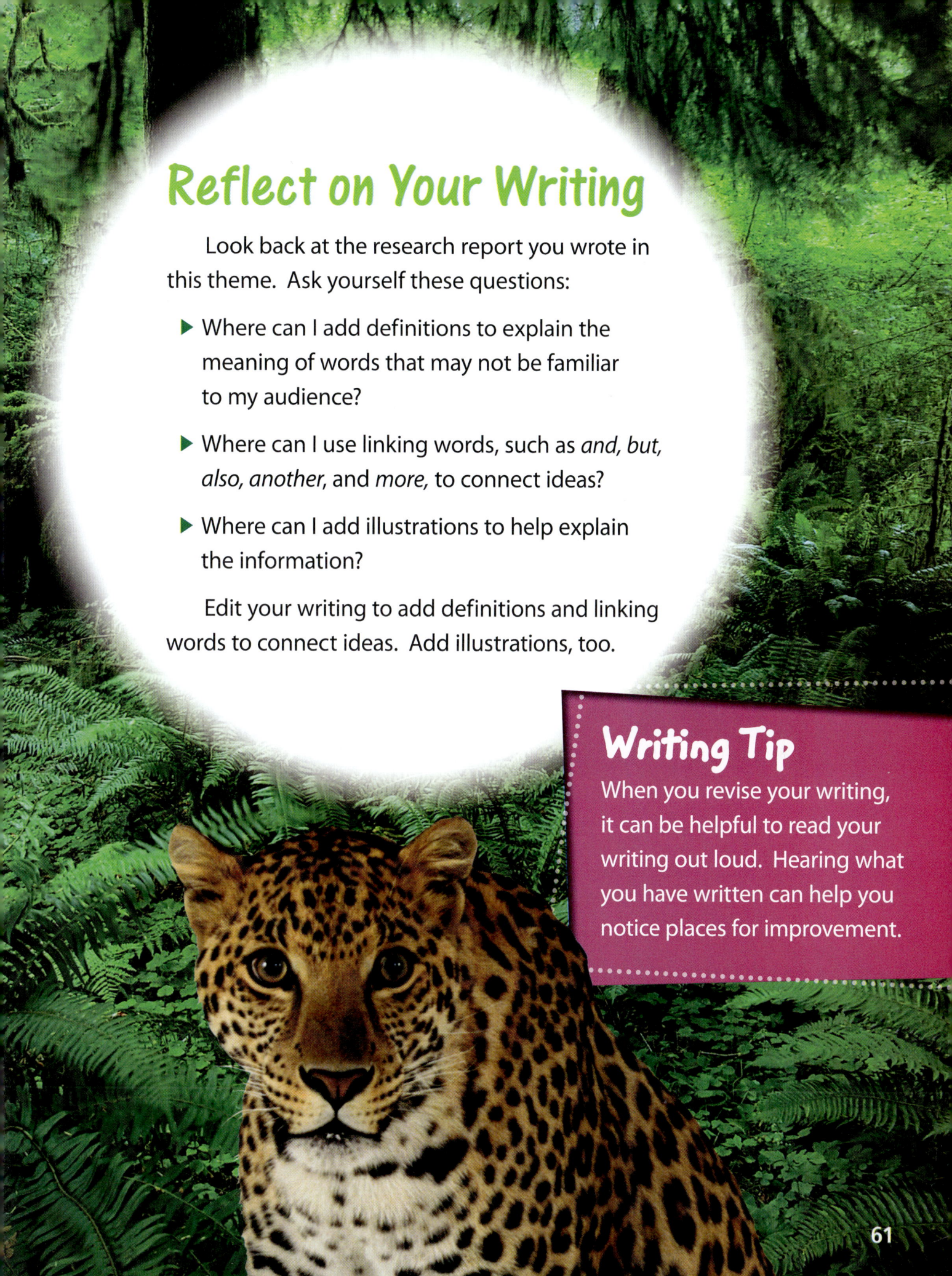

Reflect on Your Writing

Look back at the research report you wrote in this theme. Ask yourself these questions:

▶ Where can I add definitions to explain the meaning of words that may not be familiar to my audience?

▶ Where can I use linking words, such as *and, but, also, another*, and *more,* to connect ideas?

▶ Where can I add illustrations to help explain the information?

Edit your writing to add definitions and linking words to connect ideas. Add illustrations, too.

Writing Tip

When you revise your writing, it can be helpful to read your writing out loud. Hearing what you have written can help you notice places for improvement.

Theme 5
Technology Gets You There
by Judy Schmauss

People travel all the time, and they travel in many different ways. A car ride to your grandmother's home, an airplane trip for a vacation, or a bus ride to school are all ways to travel.

In earlier times there were no cars, airplanes, or even bicycles. People still traveled, but not as much as people do today. Long ago, people traveled on foot, by boat, or by horse and wagon.

Technology has changed the way people do lots of things, including how they travel. Technology has made traveling faster, easier, and safer than ever before.

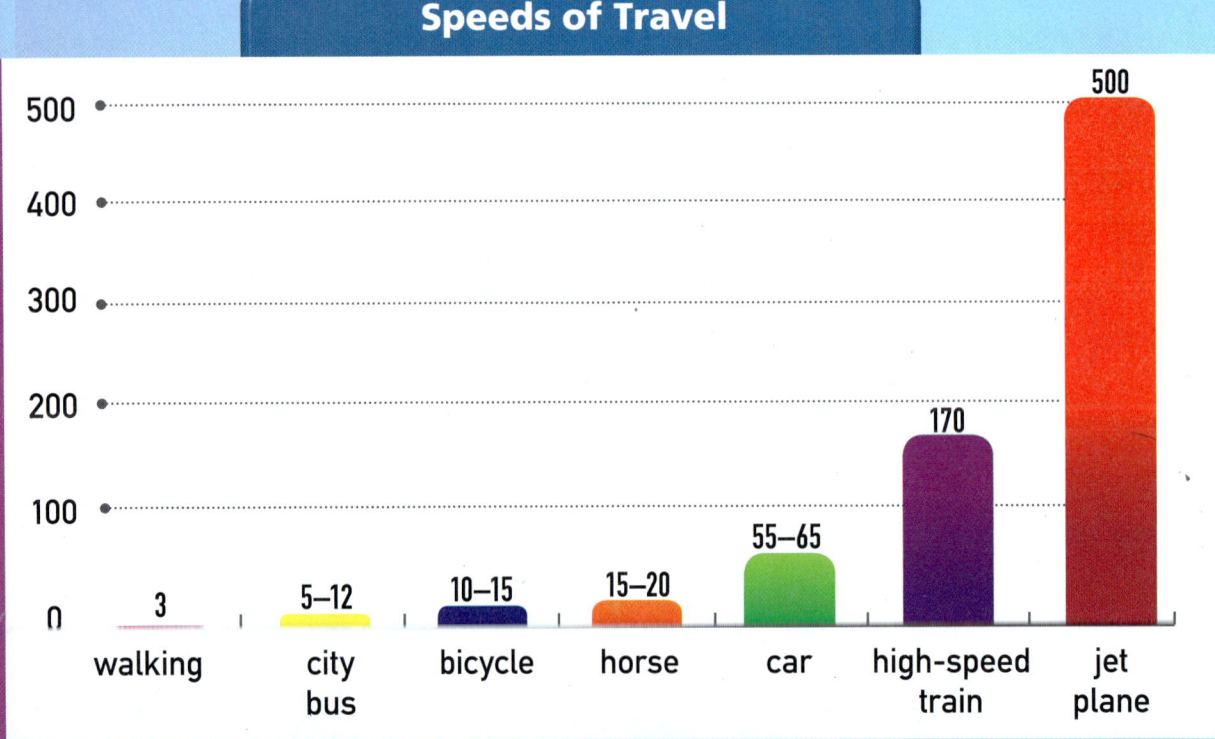

Speeds of Travel

miles per hour

- walking: 3
- city bus: 5–12
- bicycle: 10–15
- horse: 15–20
- car: 55–65
- high-speed train: 170
- jet plane: 500

The Science of Travel

Changes in travel technology are made by engineers and designers. Engineers use technology to improve something. They find solutions to problems in everyday life.

However you travel, an engineer has helped make your travel experience better. Engineers design new ways to make traveling easier, faster, and safer.

The first step for an engineer is to identify a problem, or something to be improved. Then the engineer comes up with a possible solution, or way to fix the problem. Next, he or she creates a model. The new idea is then tested to see how well it works. If it works well, you may notice it the next time you travel!

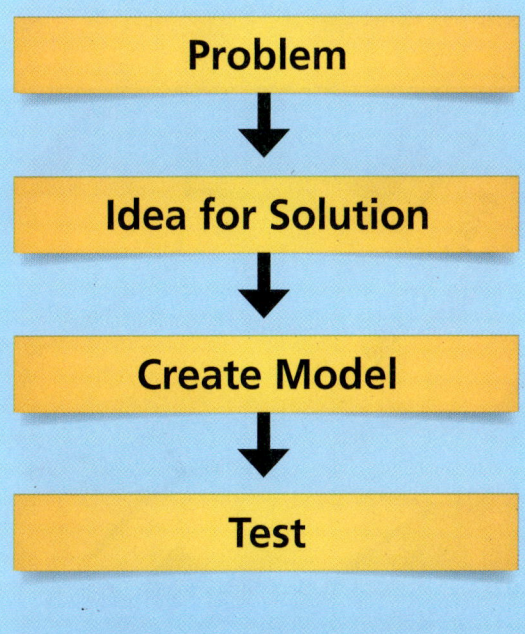

Travel by Car

How has technology changed car travel? Over time there have been lots of new cars, new roads, and new places to visit by car. New technology has changed how people find their way.

Suppose that your parents are going to drive you to a friend's house for the first time. How can you find out how long the trip will take? How can you find the best way to go?

Use a Map

Twenty years ago, a map was the easiest way to find this information. A road map shows the distance from one place to another. You look at the map and find the most direct route.

Use the Internet

Now the same information can be found on the Internet. On many websites, you simply type in your address and your friend's address. A map, distance, and directions for the trip can then be printed from the computer.

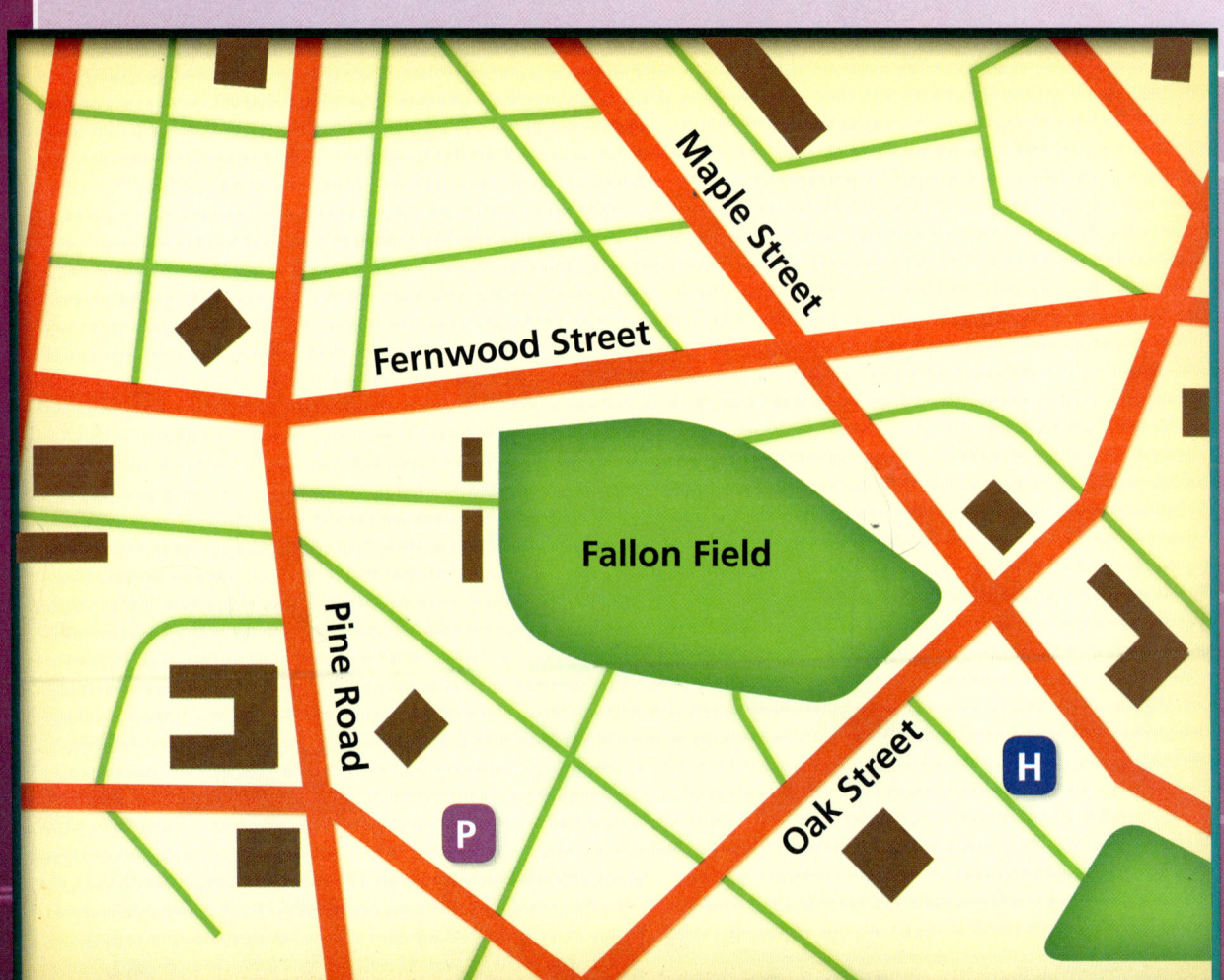

Use a GPS

A GPS (Global Positioning System) is another way to plan your car travel. With a map or website directions, drivers have to know where they are to find their way somewhere else. They have to look at a map or read directions. This is not safe when they are driving. Engineers solved these problems with the GPS.

A GPS tells you where you are. It tells you how long it's going to take to get where you want to go. It shows a driver turn-by-turn directions and speaks the directions, too. Drivers can buy for their cars GPS equipment that is a bit bigger than a cell phone. In fact, many cell phones have a GPS built right into them.

Travel by Bus

Many people ride buses to work or school. Technology has made traveling by bus easier.

Have you ever seen a "kneeling" bus? In the past, it was difficult for many people to walk up and down the high steps of a bus. Someone in a wheelchair could not ride an ordinary bus. Engineers solved the problem. They found a way to make the floor of a stopped bus kneel, or move down. People can get on and off the bus in one small step. A ramp is extended from under the floor. The ramp allows wheelchairs to move on and off the bus.

On many buses, there's no need to pay the bus driver. Riders buy a ride card at a machine. They swipe the card past a computer "eye" as they get on the bus.

Travel by Rail

For a long time, people all over the world have traveled by train and subway. One recent invention is high-speed trains. A high-speed train can go three times as fast as a regular train.

Engineers designed high-speed trains for many reasons. One reason is to move many travelers very quickly. This helps to cut traffic in crowded cities. Another reason is to save energy. High-speed trains use less energy than cars and airplanes. Another reason is that high-speed trains create less pollution than cars. This is because they use electric power. Last, computer technology helps make sure high-speed trains are even safer than normal-speed trains.

Travel by Plane

Twenty years ago, most travelers called a travel agent to find an airplane flight. The traveler picked up the ticket from the travel agent, at the airport, or from their mailbox.

Today, many travelers do it all themselves from a home computer. A few computer clicks show all the flights and prices to wherever people need to go. They choose a flight and pay for it online. Travelers can even choose the seat they want. When they get to the airport, they enter their name on a touch screen. Then they swipe a credit card or passport, and they get their ticket.

How Will Travel Change?

Now that you have read about the latest travel technology, think about how you get from place to place. Do you think it is much different than fifty or one hundred years ago? How do you think technology will change the way people travel fifty years from now?

The next time you travel—by bus, train, car, or maybe airplane—think about how your trip could be even faster, easier, or safer. Maybe you'll be the one with the next big idea in travel technology!

Picture This

Good speakers make their listeners feel, hear, see, and smell the experience they are describing. They choose their words carefully.

What words do the speakers below use to help you picture what they saw, heard, and felt on their trips?

> It was a scorching hot day so our whole family drove to the beach. I felt a cool breeze when we got there. I dug my feet deep in the sand. Foamy waves crashed over them.

> Last Saturday, my dad and I rode the bus to the museum. There were lots of fun experiments to do. There were lights flashing and wheels turning. It was loud! There was water splashing, bells ringing, and children shrieking.

Think about a travel experience you have had. It could be a trip downtown, a trip to your grandmother's house, a field trip, or something else. Describe to your classmates the place where you went and how you got there. What did you do? What did you see? What did you hear?

Before you talk about your experience, think about:

- ✹ details and words that describe your trip and how you felt.
- ✹ words and phrases that will make your audience feel as though they are with you on the trip.

As you are speaking, remember to speak clearly and in complete sentences.

When you are listening to someone else speak, remember to listen carefully so that you can ask questions when the speaker has finished.

Good writers use clear, descriptive language to tell about the thoughts, feelings, and actions of characters. Good writers use descriptive words and details to make the events and experiences come alive for their audience. As you read the paragraph below, notice the descriptive details and how the writer feels.

I had waited eagerly all week for my first train ride. I was excited as my mom and I zoomed up the train station escalator. When I reached the train platform, my eyes blinked a few times. The train was taller and longer than I expected. We raced to the train car at the front. I wanted to be the first to see everything along the way. I felt my seat rumble slightly as the train engines started.

Reflect on Your Writing

Look back at the description you wrote in this theme. Ask yourself these questions:

- Did I use words that clearly describe each character's actions?
- Did I tell how things look, sound, taste, smell, and feel?
- Did I use words that make the experience and events come alive to the reader?

If you answer no to any of the questions, edit your description.

Theme 6

A Mr. Rubbish Mood
from Judy Moody Saves the World!

by Megan McDonald
illustrated by Peter H. Reynolds

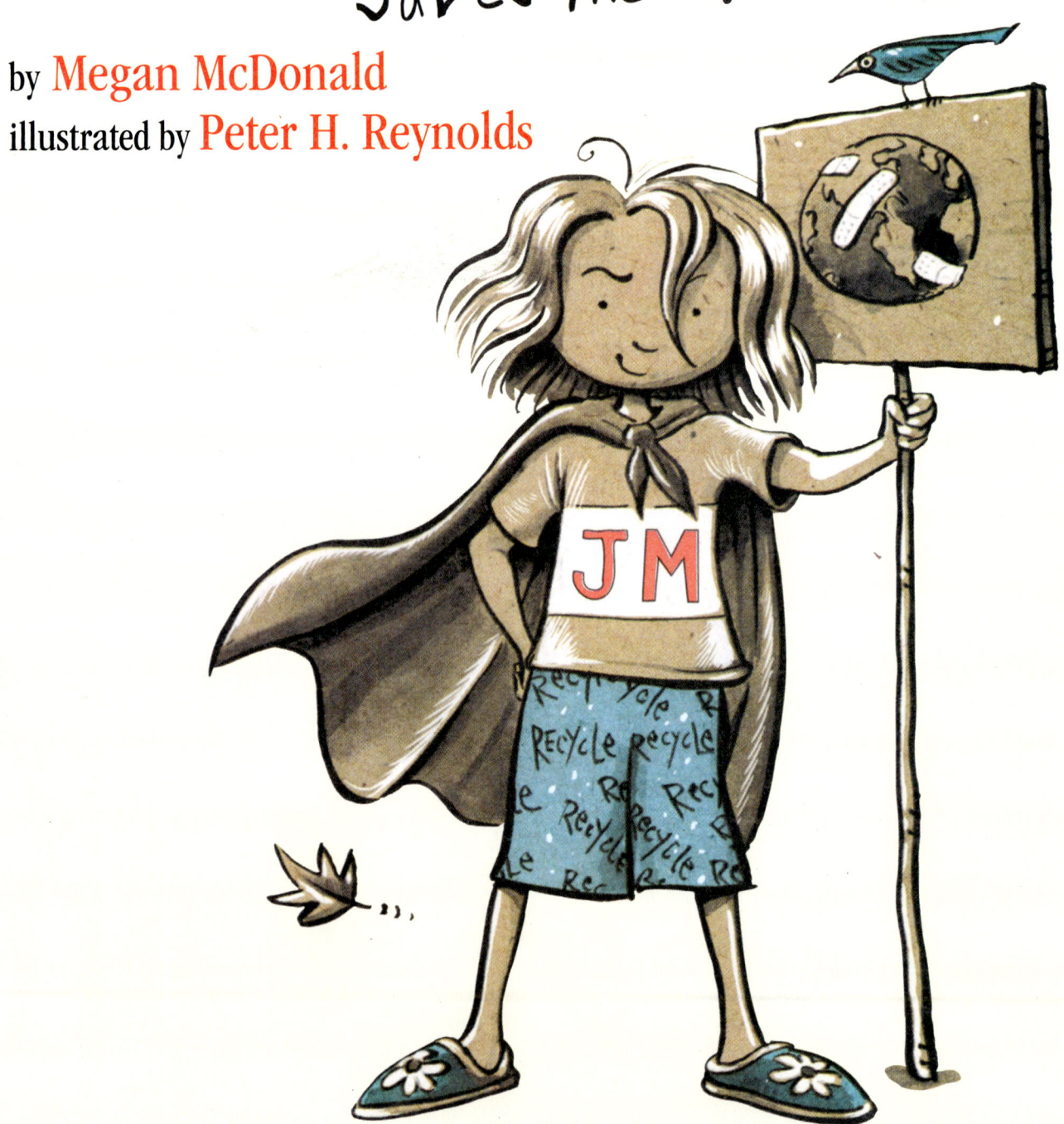

It was still dark out when Judy woke up early the next morning. She found her flashlight and notebook. Then she tiptoed downstairs to the kitchen and started to save the world.

She hoped she could save the world before breakfast. Judy wondered if other people making the world a better place had to do it quietly, and in the dark, so their parents would not wake up.

She, Judy Moody, was in a Mr. Rubbish mood. Mr. Rubbish was the Good Garbage Gremlin in her brother Stink's comic book, who built his house out of French-fry cartons and pop bottles. He recycled everything, even lollipop sticks. And he never used anything from the rain forest.

Hmmm . . . things that came from the rain forest. That would be a good place to start. Rubber came from the rain forest. And chocolate and spices and things like perfume. Even chewing gum.

Judy collected stuff from around the house and piled it on the kitchen table. Chocolate bars, brownie mix, vanilla ice cream. Her dad's coffee beans. The rubber toilet plunger. Gum from Stink's gumball machine. Her mom's lipstick from the bottom of her purse. She was so busy saving the rain forest that she didn't hear her family come into the kitchen.

"What in the world . . . ?" Mom said.

"Judy, why are you in the dark?" Dad asked, turning on the lights.

"Hey, my gumball machine!" Stink said.

Judy held out her arms to block the way. "We're not going to use this stuff anymore. It's all from the rain forest," she told them.

"Says who?" asked Stink.

"Says Mr. Rubbish. They cut down way too many trees to grow coffee and give us makeup and chewing gum. The earth is our home. We have to take action to save it. We don't need all this stuff."

"I need gum!" yelled Stink. "Give me back my gum!"

"Stink! Don't yell. Haven't you ever heard of noise pollution?"

"Is my coffee in there?" Dad asked, rubbing his hair.

"Judy? Is that ice cream? It's dripping all over the table!" Mom carried the leaky carton over to the sink.

"ZZZZ-ZZZZZ!" Judy made the sound of a chain saw cutting down trees.

"She's batty," Stink said.

Dad put the brownie mix back in the cupboard. Mom took the toilet plunger off the kitchen table and headed for the bathroom.

Time for Plan B. Project R.E.C.Y.C.L.E. She, Judy Moody, would show her family just how much they hurt the planet. Every time someone threw something away, she would write it down. She got her notebook and looked in the trash can. She wrote down:

1 orange juice can
1 inside of peanut butter jar lid
1 plastic bread bag
4 broken eggshells
smelly yucky wet coffee grounds
3 paper muffin holders
2 smooshed Scarlett O'Cherry Juice Boxes (and straws!)
½ bowl of oatmeal

"Stink! You shouldn't throw gooey old oatmeal in the trash!" Judy said.

"Dad! Tell her to quit spying on me."

"I'm a Garbage Detective!" said Judy. "*Garbologist* to you. If you want to learn what to recycle, you have to get to know your garbage."

"Here," said Stink, sticking something wet and mushy under Judy's nose. "Get to know my apple core."

"Hardee-har-har," said Judy. "Hasn't anybody in this family ever heard of the Three R's?"

"The Three R's?" asked Dad.

"Re-use. Re-cycle."

"What's the third one?" asked Stink.

"Re-fuse to talk to little brothers until they quit throwing stuff away."

"Mom! I'm not going to stop throwing stuff away just because Judy's having a trash attack."

"Look at all this stuff we throw away!" Judy said. "Did you know that one person throws away more than eight pounds of garbage a day?"

"We recycle all our glass and cans," said Mom.
"And newspapers," Dad said.
"But what about this?" said Judy, picking a plastic bag out of the trash. "This bread bag could be a purse! Or carry a library book."

"What's so great about eggshells?" asked Stink. "And smelly old ground-up coffee?"

"You can use them to feed plants. Or make compost." Just then, something in the trash caught her eye. A pile of wooden craft sticks? Judy pulled it out. "Hey! My Laura Ingalls Wilder log cabin I made in second grade!"

"It looks like a glue museum to me," said Stink.

"I'm sorry, Judy," Mom said. "I should have asked first, but we can't save everything, honey."

"Recycle it!" said Stink. "You could use it for kindling, to start a fire! Or break it down into toothpicks."

"Not funny, Stink."

"Judy, you're not even ready for school yet. Let's talk about this later," said Dad. "It's time to get dressed."

It was no use. Nobody listened to her. Judy trudged upstairs, feeling like a sloth without a tree.

"I won't wear lipstick today if it'll make you feel better," Mom called up the stairs.

"And I'll only drink half a cup of coffee," Dad said, but Judy could hardly hear him over the grinding of the rain forest coffee beans.

Her family sure knew how to ruin a perfectly good Mr. Rubbish mood. She put on her jeans and her Spotted Owl T-shirt. And to save water, she did not brush her teeth.

She clomped downstairs in a mad-at-your-whole-family mood.

"Here's your lunch," said Mom.

"Mom! It's in a paper bag!"

"What's wrong with that?" Stink asked.

"Don't you get it?" said Judy. "They cut down trees to make paper bags. Trees give shade. They help control global warming. We would die without trees. They make oxygen and help take dust and stuff out of the air."

"Dust!" said Mom. "Let's talk about cleaning your room if we're going to talk about dust."

"Mo-om!" How was she supposed to do important things like save trees if she couldn't even save her *family* tree? That did it. Judy went straight to the garage and dug out her Sleeping Beauty lunch box from kindergarten.

"Are you really going to take that baby lunch box on the bus? Where the whole world can see?" asked Stink.

"I'm riding my bike today," said Judy. "To save energy."

"See you at school, then." Stink waved his *paper-bag* lunch at her. If only she could recycle her little brother.

"Go ahead. Be a tree hater," called Judy.

Making the world a better place sure was complicated.

My Favorite Pet
My Smelly Pet
from Judy Moody

by Megan McDonald
illustrated by Peter H. Reynolds

My Favorite Pet

It was Labor Day, a no-school day. Judy looked up from her Me collage on the dining room table.

"We need a new pet," Judy announced to her family.

"A new pet? What's wrong with Mouse?" asked Mom. Mouse opened one eye.

"I have to pick MY FAVORITE PET. How can I pick my favorite when I only have one?"

"Pick Mouse," said Mom.

"Mouse is so old, and she's afraid of everything. Mouse is a lump that purrs."

"You're NOT thinking of a dog, I hope," said Dad. Mouse jumped off the chair and stretched.

"Mouse would definitely not like that," said Judy.

"How about a goldfish?" asked Stink. Mouse rubbed up against Judy's leg.

"Mouse would like that too much," Judy said. "I was thinking of a two-toed sloth."

"Right," said Stink.

"They're neat," said Judy. She showed Stink its picture in her rain forest magazine.

"See? They hang upside down all day. They even sleep upside down."

"You're upside down," said Stink.

"What do they eat?" asked Dad.

"It says here they eat leaf-cutter ants and fire-bellied toads," Judy read.

"That should be easy," said Stink.

"Tell you what, Judy," said Dad. "Let's take a ride over to the pet store. I'm not saying we'll get a sloth, but it's always fun to look around. Maybe it'll even help me think of a five-letter word for fish that starts with *M* for my crossword puzzle."

"Let's all go," said Mom.

When they arrived at Fur & Fangs, Judy saw snakes and parrots, hermit crabs and guppies. She even saw a five-letter fish word beginning with *M*—a black molly.

"Do you have any two-toed sloths?" she asked the pet store lady.

"Sorry. Fresh out," said the lady.

"How about a newt or a turtle?" asked Dad.

"Did you see the hamsters?" asked Mom.

"Never mind," said Judy. "There's nothing from the rain forest here."

"Maybe they have a stinkbug," Stink said.

"One's enough," said Judy, narrowing her eyes at Stink. They picked out a squeaky mouse toy for Mouse. When they went to pay for it, Judy noticed a green plant with teeth sitting on the counter. "What's that?" she asked the pet store lady.

"A Venus flytrap," the lady said. "It's not an animal, but it doesn't cost much, and it's easy to take care of. See these things that look like mouths with teeth? Each one closes like a trap door. It eats bugs around the house. Like flies and ants, that sort of thing. You can feed it a little raw hamburger too."

"Rare," said Judy Moody.

"Cool," said Stink.

"Good idea," said Mom.

"Sold," said Dad.

Judy set her new pet on her desk, where the angle of sunlight hit it just right. Mouse watched from the bottom bunk, with one eye open.

"I can't wait to take my new pet to school tomorrow for Share and Tell," Judy told Stink. "It's just like a rare plant from the rain forest."

"It is?" Stink asked.

"Sure," said Judy. "Just think. There could be a medicine hiding right here in these funny green teeth. When I'm a doctor, I'm going to study plants like this and discover cures for ucky diseases."

"What are you going to name it?" asked Stink.

"I don't know yet," said Judy.

"You could call it Bughead, since it likes bugs."

"Nah," said Judy.

Judy watered her new pet. She sprinkled Gro-Fast on the soil. When Stink left, she sang songs to it. "I know an old lady who swallowed a fly. . . ." She sang till the old lady swallowed a horse.

She still couldn't think of a good name. Rumpelstiltskin? Too long. Thing? Maybe.

"Stink!" she called. "Go get me a fly."

"How am I going to catch a fly?" asked Stink.

"One fly. I'll give you a dime." Stink ran down to the window behind the couch and brought back a fly.

"Gross! That fly is dead."

"It was going to be dead in a minute anyway."

Judy scooped up the dead fly with the tip of her ruler and dropped it into one of the mouths. In a flash, the trap closed around the fly. Just like the pet store lady said.

"Rare!" said Judy.

"Snap! Trap!" Stink said, adding sound effects.

"Go get me an ant. A live one this time."

Here's one... ...a real beauty!

Here anty, anty! No way!

Snap! Trap! Urp!

Stink wanted to see the Venus flytrap eat again, so he got his sister an ant. "Snap! Trap!" said Judy and Stink when another trap closed.

"Double rare," Judy said.

"Stink, go catch me a spider or something."

"I'm tired of catching bugs," said Stink.

"Then go ask Mom or Dad if we have any raw hamburger."

Stink frowned.

"Please, pretty please with bubble-gum ice cream on top?" Judy begged. Stink didn't budge. "I'll let you feed it this time."

Stink ran to the kitchen and came back with a hunk of raw hamburger. He plopped a big glob of hamburger into an open trap.

"That's way too much!" Judy yelled, but it was too late. The mouth snap-trapped around it, hamburger oozing out of its teeth. In a blink, the whole arm drooped, collapsing in the dirt.

"You killed it! You're in trouble, Stink. MOM! DAD!" Judy called.

Judy showed her parents what happened. "Stink killed my Venus flytrap!"

"I didn't mean to," said Stink. "The trap closed really fast!"

"It's not dead. It's digesting," said Dad.

"The jaws will probably open by tomorrow morning," said Mom.

"Maybe it's just sleeping or something," said Stink.

"Or something," said Judy.

My Smelly Pet

Tomorrow morning came. The jaws were still closed. Judy tried teasing it with a brand new ant. "Here you go," she said in her best squeaky baby voice. "You like ants, don't you?" The jaws did not open one tiny centimeter. The plant did not move one trigger hair.

Judy gave up. She carefully lodged the plant in the bottom of her backpack. She'd take it to school, stinky, smelly glob of hamburger and all.

On the bus, Judy showed Rocky her new pet. "I couldn't wait to show everybody how it eats. Now it won't even move. And it smells."

"Open Sesame!" said Rocky, trying some magic words. Nothing happened.

"Maybe," said Rocky, "the bus will bounce it open."

"Maybe," said Judy. But even the bouncing of the bus did not make her new pet open up.

"If this thing dies, I'm stuck with Mouse for MY FAVORITE PET," Judy said.

Mr. Todd said first thing, "Okay, class, take out your Me collage folders. I'll pass around old magazines, and you can spend the next half-hour cutting out pictures for your collages. You still have over three weeks, but I'd like to see how everybody's doing."

Her Me collage folder! Judy had been so busy with her new pet, she had forgotten to bring her folder to school.

Judy Moody sneaked a peek at Frank Pearl's folder. He had cut out pictures of macaroni (favorite food?), ants (favorite pet?), and shoes. Shoes? Frank Pearl's best friend was a pair of shoes?

Judy looked down at the open backpack under her desk. The jaws were still closed. Now her whole backpack was smelly. Judy took the straw from her juice box and poked at the Venus flytrap. No luck. It would never open in time for Share and Tell!

"Well?" Frank asked.

"Well, what?"

"Are you going to come?"

"Where?"

"My birthday party. A week from Saturday. All the boys from our class are coming. And Adrian and Sandy from next door."

Judy Moody did not care if the president himself was coming. She sniffed her backpack. It stunk like a skunk!

"What's in your backpack?" Frank asked.

"None of your beeswax," Judy said.

"It smells like dead tuna fish!" Frank Pearl said. Judy hoped her Venus flytrap would come back to life and bite Frank Pearl before he ever had another birthday.

Mr. Todd came over. "Judy, you haven't cut out any pictures. Do you have your folder?"

"I did—I mean—it was—then—well—no," said Judy. "I got a new pet last night."

"Don't tell me," said Mr. Todd. "Your new pet ate your Me collage folder."

"Not exactly. But it did eat one dead fly and one live ant. And then a big glob of . . ."

"Next time try to remember to bring your folder to school, Judy. And please, everyone, keep homework away from animals!"

"My new pet's not an animal, Mr. Todd," Judy said. "And it doesn't eat homework. Just bugs and raw hamburger." She pulled the Venus flytrap from her backpack. Judy could not believe her eyes! Its arm was no longer droopy. The stuck trap was now wide open, and her plant was looking hungry.

"It's MY FAVORITE PET," said Judy. "Meet Jaws!"

Activity Central

Defined Online

In the chapter "My Favorite Pet," Judy asks Stink to get some bugs. At first Stink does not budge. If you don't know the meaning of the word *budge,* you can use an online dictionary to look up the meaning.

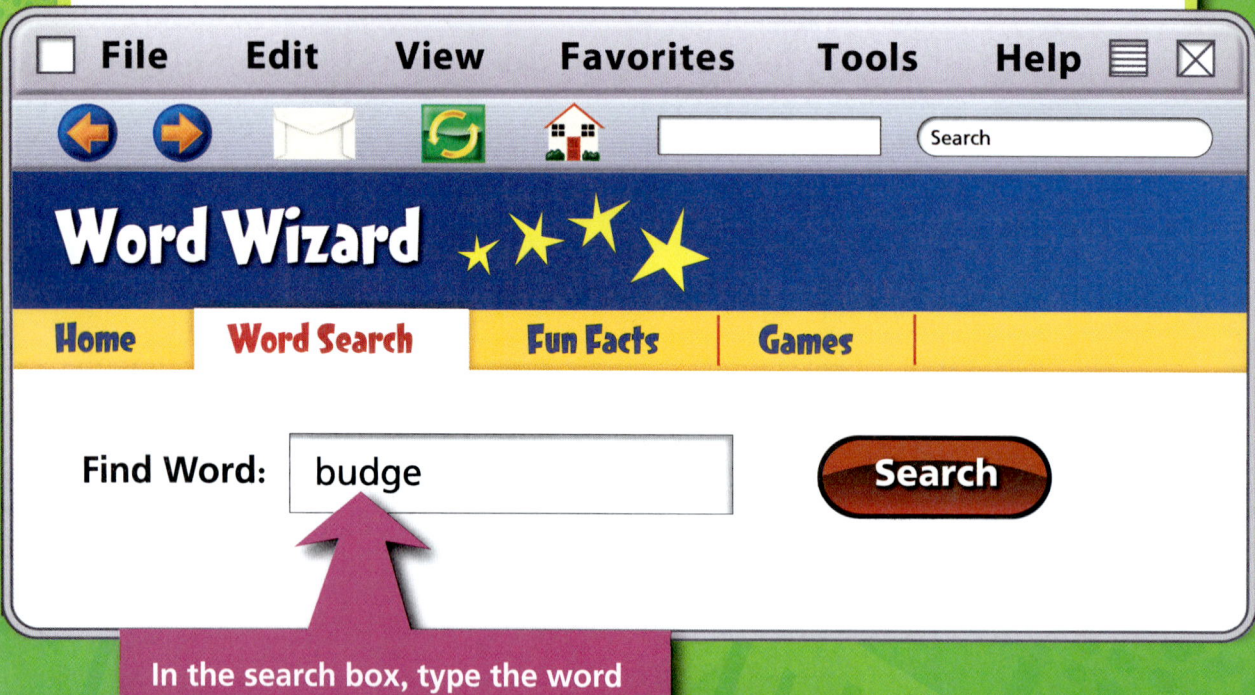

In the search box, type the word you want to look up. Click on the "Search" button or press the "Enter" key on the keyboard.

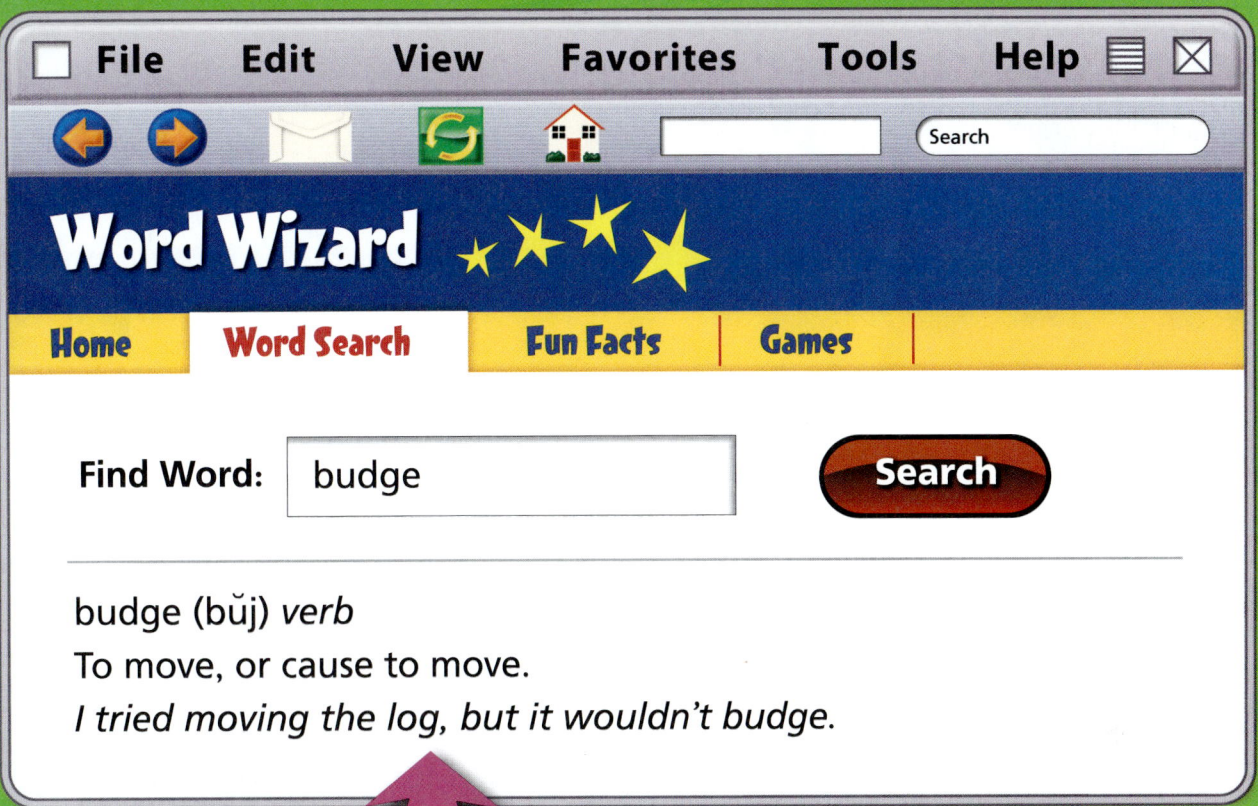

Read the entry to find out what the word means. If there is more than one entry for a word, choose the meaning that matches the way the word is used in the selection.

Read the sentences. Use an online dictionary to find the meanings of the underlined words.

1. When they finished their meal at the restaurant, they paid for it at the counter.

2. The old mansion had a trap door.

3. The leaves of the plant were droopy.

4. The trigger hairs on the plant swayed toward the insect.

Your Turn

Linked Together

When you write a persuasive essay, you try to convince your readers to agree with your opinion. Use linking words and phrases, such as *because*, *since*, and *for example*, to connect your opinion to your reasons.

How does this writer make his opinion stronger? What is the linking word?

> I think everyone should recycle bottles and cans because it makes less waste and helps the environment.

Don't forget to leave your readers with something to remember! Sum up your ideas in a strong ending.

> Materials that we recycle don't end up in our oceans and rivers. This makes the environment cleaner and healthier for all life.